INDIANS,

'JACKS,

AND PINES

A History of Saginaw
by
Stuart D. Gross

Illustrated
by
Ralph A. Misiak and Samuel Carter Jr.

To
Helen M. Tewes

TABLE OF CONTENTS

PREFACE

This history of Saginaw leans heavily on research done by the late Fred Dustin, Saginaw's best known historian, and articles that have appeared in The Saginaw News.

Mr. Dustin's work is "The History of Saginaw." Segments of Saginaw history that are not detailed in this account are detailed in Mr. Dustin's book, and the serious student of Saginaw history is encouraged to read that volume.

Nor is this a complete history. It was not intended to be. Rather it is to present the high spots of Saginaw's development, and every effort has been made to choose for illustration the colorful events that made Saginaw known as the lumbering capital of the world.

Histories of early America sometimes make it appear that the white man is the villain and the Indian the innocent victim of the settling of the west.

Neither viewpoint is correct.

The Indian was primitive. He lived in the stone age with bows and arrows as weapons. The white man who came to these shores was the product of a civilization that had learned to read and write, and his science had developed to the point where he could till the land and produce food far easier and in greater quantities than the Indian.

This history does not attempt to explain why the white man displaced the Indian. Neither will it attempt to defend the Indian. It is ridiculous to think the Indian could go on and on living as he did in this country and never be displaced. Unfortunately for our peace of conscience, the deed was done by our great-grandfathers. It is too near home for all of us to try to justify what happened.

Nor will this history shed tears on the cutting of the great pine forests. The pine was here to cut. But we must admit, our great-grandfathers wasted the pine. With careful management the pine could have been harvested without complete destruction of the forests.

Saginaw's history is robust and colorful. We hope this history reflects some of that color and robustiousness.

Stuart D. Gross

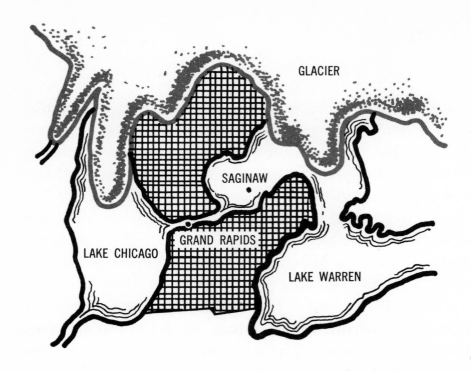

GLACIER

SAGINAW

LAKE CHICAGO

GRAND RAPIDS

LAKE WARREN

CHAPTER 1

BEFORE THE WHITE MAN

In the beginning it wasn't known as Saginaw.

Nor were the Indians, those master hunters, the first to live here.

There were people living here 13,000 years ago. Their crude stone implements have been found in sandy graves near St. Charles in Saginaw County.

Nor was the land always as you see it today. Some 50,000 years ago it was covered by water. This has been called by geologists as the Huronic Sea or Lake Warren. What now is Lake Michigan geologists named Lake Chicago.

At the time of Lake Warren and Lake Chicago, you could have journeyed from Saginaw to Lake Michigan, straight across the State, in a canoe. The route would have been almost a straight line, along a glacial spillway that carried westward the outflow from Lake Warren.

This lake embraced in a single great basin what now are known as Lakes St. Clair and Erie, the southern part of Lake Huron and much of eastern Michigan and southeastern Ontario.

As the huge glaciers advanced and retreated over the centuries, the contours of the land were gradually changed, leaving it much as you see it today. The spillway dried up, but its original bed with westward flowing water was to intrigue men who came later to settle Saginaw. They dreamed of a ship canal across the waist of Michigan that would tie the Saginaw, Shiawassee, Bad, Maple, and Grand Rivers together. And they made an attempt to build such a canal.

The early shores of Lake Warren are still marked by sand deposits visible in Monroe, Washtenaw, Wayne, Oakland, Macomb, St. Clair, Sanilac, Huron, Tuscola, Saginaw, Bay, Arenac, Gladwin, Midland, Isabella, and Gratiot Counties.

Some of these sand deposits, ground fine by the glaciers and smoothed by hundreds and hundreds of years of wind, have been found valuable for the foundry businesses that settled in Saginaw. One of these sand pits is in Tuscola County, between Millington and Caro, another is visible from an automobile along Highway M-46, east of Saginaw and just beyond Richville.

The glaciers also left rich lands that produced great quanties of natural food for the Indians — black walnuts, beechnuts, butternuts, red and black cherries, and black berries. The sap from the maple trees was boiled to make maple sugar, one of the few luxuries of Indian life.

The pin, or wild potato, from which Pinconning in Bay County takes its name, was found along the streams. Wild rice grew in the shallow waters of the Shiawassee River, and served not only as food for the Indian but also attracted the ducks and geese the Indian hunted.

The rivers were the highways for the Indians; it is easy to understand why the Indians congregated here. The Saginaw River which empties into Saginaw Bay is formed by the Tittabawassee, Shiawassee, Cass, and Flint Rivers.

From Saginaw an Indian could travel by canoe deep into the Thumb area or into the middle of lower Michigan. He also could go down the Saginaw to Saginaw Bay and eastward to the Atlantic Ocean. Today great ships from foreign countries follow this same route — up the St. Lawrence River, across Lake Ontario, Lake Erie, up Lake Huron to Saginaw Bay and the shipping docks of the industries that now line the shores of Saginaw River.

The Sauk Indians were among the first known Indian tribes to settle here. But soon another tribe of Indians, the fierce Chippewas, made war on them.

The Chippewas planned their attack with care. The chiefs met on an island in the Straits of Mackinac. After several days of council talks, the chiefs sent out war parties against the Sauks.

The Indian warriors traveled by canoes down Lake Huron and into Saginaw Bay. They hid along the shore in the daytime to keep from being seen by any wandering Sauk brave out hunting.

The surprise was complete. The Sauk Indians were all but exterminated. An island in the Saginaw River was so covered with the dead it became known as Skull Island. Today it is called Crow Island.

The Chippewas gave Saginaw its name. They called it "Saugee-an-te-nah-ke-wat" which means "where the Saugee (Sauk) were." The name Saginaw had to pass through many more different spellings before it reached its final form.

Although the Sauks were defeated and driven away, the Chippewas for years lived in fear of them. There arose the legend of "The Avenging Sauk." It was told around the campfires and in the wigwams so often and with such detail that the Chippewas came to believe it.

As the legend goes, one Sauk brave was killed in the attack trying to defend his sweetheart. Later, the Chippewas claimed to see the ghost of this brave walk from the forest. The ghost would stand in a clearing near the village and stare accusingly at the Chippewas.

So great was the fear of this spectre that entire villages would flee in panic. Some of the early white men made use of this fear to frighten Indians from the villages. While the Indians were hiding in the forest, the white men would loot furs from the wigwams.

CHAPTER 2

INDIAN LIFE

One of the first Indian camps in the Saginaw area was built at a place known to the Indians as "O-zhaw-wash-quah," or Green Point. Green Point is in the southern part of Saginaw where the Shiawassee and Tittabawassee Rivers join to form the Saginaw River.

Here thousands of Indian arrow heads, spear points, pottery, totem symbols, ax heads, and Indian scrapers have been found.

Trails led from this village to other points in Michigan. Two went south to Detroit. One of these trails went by way of present day Bridgeport and Flint. Another by way of Chesaning and Owosso. Still another trail led west to Lake Michigan following Bad River, Saginaw County tributary of the Shiawassee, and the Grand River which empties into Lake Michigan.

One of the most famous of the trails was known as the Mackinaw Trail. This trail snaked through the forests from Detroit to Sault Ste. Marie, and followed, in part, present Mackinaw Road. It passed through or near the present sites of Royal Oak, Pontiac, Clarkston, Grand Blanc, Flint, Moresville, Bridgeport, Saginaw, Freeland, Midland and Edenville.

At Edenville the Saginaw trail continued north and west to Grand Traverse Bay, while the Mackinaw Trail went north through or near Highwood, Secord, West Branch, Damon, Luzerne, Red Oak, Atlanta, Tower, Manning, and Cheboygan to Mackinaw City. Crossing the Mackinac Straits to St. Ignace the route followed to Sault Ste. Marie.

(This was the historic Mackinaw Trail. However, in 1959 the Michigan Legislature gave the Mackinaw Trail designation to Highway 131 on the western side of the State. The logic for this is not known.)

The Michigan Indian did not live in a tepee. The tepee was the home of the Indians of the Great Plains — the Dakota, Sioux, Comanche and Crow.

In Michigan the Indians' home was an oval wigwam. It was shaped like a big beaver house. Its frame was made by tieing small trees together and it was covered with bark. In the center of this wigwam a hole was dug in the ground about two feet across and a foot or so deep. Stones as large as a man's two fists were put at the bottom and a fire was built on top.

In cold weather, these stones held the heat through the night. A small smokehole was left in the roof of the wigwam. When well built these wigwams were fairly comfortable.

The Indian was constantly moving according to the season of the year. In Summer, he built his camp on high ground, usually on a river bank, so breezes would help blow away the pesky mosquitoes and black flies. For Winter, he moved to the lower grounds along the river bottom. There the dense forest helped protect him from Winter's winds.

Just as people do today, the Indian liked to live with friends, and family ties were strong. They lived together in clans, and each clan had a symbol. Thus developed the Beaver Clan, the Deer Clan, the Turtle Clan. The clans showed who they were by chipping the figures of their totem from stone or carving it from wood. Sometimes the symbols were polished to make them very beautiful. There were many of these clans in Michigan. Remains of 150 village sites have been found in Saginaw County alone.

The largest village site was on Green Point. Other sites have been found along river banks. The Indian built on high river banks so he could see long distances in all directions. He had to be constantly alert to an attack by an enemy.

Some Indian village sites have been located by farmers plowing their fields. The plow point may turn up arrow heads or pieces of pottery, and if enough of these are found it can be assumed that this particular location once was the site of an Indian village.

Indians also buried items with their dead, and Indian burial mounds are a rich source of artifacts of Indian life. One of the largest of these mounds in Saginaw was at the site of the present City Water Works Plant on Rust Drive.

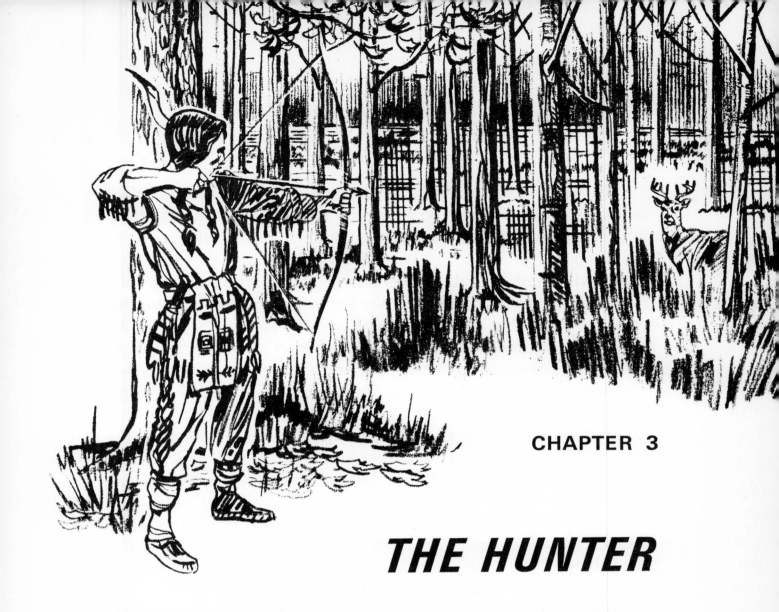

CHAPTER 3

THE HUNTER

An Indian couldn't afford to be lazy. There was too much to do keeping food in the wigwam and tanning animal skins for clothing.

The Indian's chief weapons were the bow and arrow, a flint knife, and a stone hatchet. The bow was made of ash, hickory or oak wood. The arrows were of "arrow-wood," a type of shoot that came from sheepberry or cranberry bushes. The straightest of these stems were used, tipped with an arrow-point chipped from stone. Much of the stone for the arrow heads and the other crude tools came from the great limestone deposits at Bay Port on Saginaw Bay in Huron County.

Although game was plentiful, it was not easy to kill. The bow and arrow was not too good as a weapon. The hunter had to get close to his quarry before he could be sure of hitting it in a vital spot.

So the Indian stalked his game. He watched at the salt licks, and hid along runways or lay in ambush along the streams where he knew the animals came to drink. In Winter he could follow deer tracks. It wasn't unusual for an Indian to follow a deer for two or three days until the animal became so exhausted it no longer could run. The Indian then could get close enough to shoot.

Fishing was an easier way for the Indian to get a meal. The streams were filled with catfish, pike, large- and small-mouth bass, walleyes, suckers, and even the great sturgeon in the Saginaw River.

One way was to trap the fish. The Indians put baskets or nets in the water, and then built fences in the stream to guide the fish into the trap. Sometimes, however, they waded into the streams and actually drove the fish into the nets.

A more common way was to spear the fish. Fish spears made of bones were used widely by the Indians. During the spring run of suckers it was easy for the Indian to stand in the stream and spear as many fish as he wanted.

One of the Indians big problems was the preserving of his foods. He had no corner grocery, no refrigerator, no freezer to keep meat fresh. When he killed a deer, he ate as much as he could at once. This was especially true in warm weather, when meat spoils quickly.

But the Indian did have a way to preserve foods that would keep. He dug pits in dry soil where the drainage was good. The pits were carefully lined with bark, and would keep perfectly

not only corn but nuts, dried berries, plums, maple sugar and wild rice. The white man called these "corn pits."

The Indian also dried and pounded lean meat for preservation, and packed it away in sacks of hide. This is called pemmican, and the Indian could carry this dried meat in a pouch as he hunted in the woods.

The animals the Indians killed provided their clothing. The skin was tanned. This process involved scraping the hide to remove all particles of flesh, and then treating it with salt and by drying. Deer hide was used most often, but elk, bear, beaver and otter skins also were popular.

The men and women made their own clothings. It was a slow process. There were no sewing machines, nothing resembling scissors. Bone awls were used in place of needles. The tough sinews from the animals were used as thread, and porcupine quills as ornaments.

The typical costume for a man was a shirt, which hung to his hips. There was a hood that could be drawn over the head in cold weather. He also wore a breech cloth, and long leggings tied to a belt around the waist.

The women wore dresses with loose sleeves ending at the elbows and taken in at the waist with a belt. They, too, wore leggings.

The free edges of these clothes were left long and were fringed by cutting into narrow strips. This was not for ornament. The fringing prevented the skin from puckering and wrinkling when it became wet. White hunters were quick to copy the idea.

In warm weather, the men sometimes went without shirts and leggings. But mosquitoes and flies were pestiferous and the braves often wore their leather shirts for protection.

The use of feathers was not common. Occasionally eagle feathers were worn much the same as a soldier wears a Medal of Honor or other decorations. A warrior who had scalped an enemy wore two feathers. If he had taken a wounded prisoner, five feathers were arranged in a certain design as a head decoration. The elaborate head gears of feathers were used by the Sioux of the plains but never by the Chippewa.

Smoking was enjoyed by the Indians. They fashioned their pipes from stone, but more often made them of pottery. The Indian had learned the secret of making pottery for cooking, and was skillful in turning out vessels for water containers and others tempered for use over fire.

Eating utensils like the knife, fork and spoon were unknown in the wigwam. A stout branch from a tree was used to lift the meat from the fire. When the food had cooled, the Indian ate with his fingers.

Many an Indian brave must have laughed to himself at the strange ways of the white man who did not know the ways of nature.

Some Indian Names

Bad River — The two branches of this river are now called the North and South branches. They empty into the Shiawassee River. The Chippewas gave each branch a name. The South branch was called Maw-tchi-sebe, which literally means Bad River because of the difficulty in navigating it. The North branch was Mis-a-box or White Rabbit, so called because of the many snowshoe or white rabbits on the banks.

Maw-kwa-sebe — This means Bear River which enters the Shiawassee River in St. Charles Township.

Na-da-way — This means "I bring him in a canoe." It also is the translation for the Cass River.

Crow Island — In the treaty of 1819, certain lands including an island in the Saginaw River were reserved for Kish-kaw-ko, the Crow, said to be a minor chief of the Chippewas. This bit of land still bears his name. The island also has been known as Skull Island, dating back to the savage battle when the Chippewas drove the Sauk from the Saginaw Valley.

Cheboyganing Creek — "Place of the big pipe." This may be an incorrect interpretation. Other authorities say that Cheboygan means a "sound like that of the passing of a needle through fabric or skin."

Sebewaing — Means "little river."

Shiawassee — Means "green river" taken from the vast green marshes above its mouth.

Swan Creek — An erroneous rendering of She-sheeb-se-be, all e's pronounced as in eat. It's true meaning is "Duck Creek."

Tittabawassee — A corruption and shortening of an Indian phrase signifying "the river that follows the shore." Note its course on the map making about the same curve that Saginaw Bay shows.

Chesaning — "Big Rock Place." When the first white settlers arrived in this vicinity there was a great limestone rock in the river, but it later was broken up and used for making lime. Also at some distance eastward there still remains a huge boulder which may have had its part in the Indian designation. This has been, supposedly, the "Chesaning Rock."

CHAPTER 4

THE WHITE MAN COMES

The white man came to Michigan in 1701 and established Fort Ponchartrain, which later became Detroit. It was to be another 114 years before the first white man settled permanently at what now is Saginaw, only 90 miles north.

Michigan, being a peninsula, was out of the path of the great westward push of civilization from the East Coast. The pioneers traveled west primarily through Ohio and Indiana to the Mississippi River. Detroit and Chicago were thriving cities before the Indians in the central part of the Lower Peninsula were aware their way of life was to change.

In 1807 the treaty with the Ottawas was signed in Detroit, and the name of Saginaw appeared for the first time:

"The United States . . . further stipulates to furnish the said Indians with two blacksmiths, one to reside with the Chippewas at Saguina. . . . ."

However, there is no evidence the blacksmith ever came.

With this treaty the Ottowas, Potowatomies, Wyandots, and Chippewas ceded a great section of southeast Michigan. This was the first large land settlement between the Indians and whites of Michigan territory, and was the entering wedge that eventually was to turn all of Michigan over to the white settlers.

The land remaining to the Indians was an odd shaped piece with Saginaw about the geographic center. Into this happy hunting ground of virgin forest, abundant game, and one of the last strongholds of Indian life in Michigan came Louis Campau in the fall of 1815.

He wasn't the first white man here, but he was the first to stay. The Saginaw country was mentioned vaguely in writings of Jesuit priests in papers termed "The Jesuit Relations." But there is no actual proof the Jesuits ever visited here. In the days of their explorations, the route of travel to the upper Great Lakes was through Georgian Bay, some two hundred miles northeast of Saginaw. A white man, Francois Trombley, did visit the Saginaw area in 1792, but his stay was brief.

Campau, the nephew of a wealthy Detroit merchant who dealt largely in furs, was in his middle twenties when his uncle sent him to Saginaw as a fur trader.

Campau came to Saginaw in a sailing vessel. He built himself a log trading house on a point of high river bank near the present intersection of Hamilton and Clinton Streets. Fur trading was big business in those days. The furs purchased from the Indians were sent to market in the East and to Europe. Although Campau was the first white fur trader to establish in Saginaw, other fur traders were active in the area and competition was keen.

Campau's post quickly became a center of activity along the Saginaw River. He had a pleasant personality, and the Indians liked and trusted him. This was a genuine tribute, because there were many dishonest traders.

A common practice among traders was to give a gun for a pile of beaver pelts as high as the gun was long. Some traders had cheap flintlocks made with barrels six feet long. It took a lot of beaver pelts to make a pile that high. But the gun was no good, and few Indians let themselves be cheated more than once.

Campau was firmly established at Saginaw by 1819. By this time the land-hungry whites were pressuring the Federal Government to take over all lands remaining to the Indians in Michigan. The whites wanted the Indians to move west, beyond the Mississippi River.

General Lewis Cass, one of the heroes of the War of 1812, was governor of Michigan Territory at that time and also served as superintendent of Indian affairs for the Federal Government. He was thirty-six, and highly respected by the government. He was commissioned by the government to negotiate with the Indians at Saginaw to acquire for the United States the Indian land.

General Cass asked Campau to prepare for the great pow-wow with the Indians. Runners were sent out to notify the tribes of the meeting. The time for the talks was set for the middle of September 1819. But Gen. Cass, in reviewing past

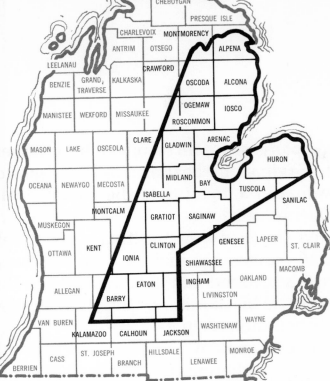

treaties with the Indians, found there were some important details that had not been followed by the government.

In the treaty of 1807, the government had promised to pay each year to the Chippewas $1,666.66 for use of their lands ceded in that treaty. This payment never had been made. Cass realized if he hoped to talk the Indians into another treaty, the terms of the other one had to be met.

He couldn't wait to send word by courier to the government in Washington. So, on his own, he borrowed the money from Detroit bankers, and then wrote to the Secretary of War, John Calhoun:

"It would be hopeless to expect a favorable result of the proposed treaty unless the annuities previously due are discharged," Cass wrote. "Under these circumstances, I have felt myself embarrassed and no course has been left me but to procure the amount of the Chippewa annuity upon my private responsibility. By the liberal conduct of the directors of the bank at this place, I have succeeded. I trust the receipt of a draft will soon relieve me from the situation in which I am placed, and enable me to perform my promise to the bank."

Gen. Cass sent a company of infantry under his brother, Capt. Charles L. Cass, to Saginaw by boat as a military guard. The general, himself, went to Saginaw over the Indian trail, arrived on September 10.

Campau had prepared the pow-wow meeting place excellently. A spacious Council House that included a platform of logs elevated a foot above the ground had been built. Here the general was to sit. Big logs, the bark still on them, were rolled into the house as seats for the Indian chiefs.

Not many Indians were present when Gen. Cass arrived, so runners were sent to notify the missing chiefs and tribal leaders. Cass, however, did not wait for the tardy ones, but opened treaty talks at once. During the conference, which lasted several days, between 1,500 and 4,000 persons were present, most of them Indians. Some white traders also attended.

Cass spoke through an interpreter. He told the Indians how the Great White Father in Washington wanted to take care of them. "The wild game is getting scarce," he said. "The Great White Father wants you to give up hunting. He wants you to live in one place and become farmers. He wants to give you land beyond the Mississippi River."

The Indians were primitive and uncivilized, but they knew what they wanted, and they didn't want to move out of Michigan beyond the Mississippi. They wanted to stay on their hunting grounds. Chief Ogemaw, who lived at what is now Midland, spoke for the Indians. He told Gen. Cass the Indians wouldn't move away, and the first session ended on this announcement.

Realizing he had no hope of convincing the Indians they should get out of Michigan so the white man could move in, Gen. Cass softened his demands. He told the Indians that if they would sign the treaty they could continue to hunt in the forests. The Indians thought they had won a victory, and on September 24, 1819, the treaty was signed by Gen. Cass and 114 chiefs.

Among the provisions of the treaty was one that the Government would pay the Chippewa nation $1,000 in silver every year. Another was the reservation of land to John, James, and Peter Riley, sons of James V. S. Riley and a Chippewa woman, Menaw-cum-ego-qua. The Rileys had given the government aid in the War of 1812, and also had served as guide to Gen. Cass in Detroit. This aid, no doubt, was the cause of the generous gifts of land. John's land was within the corporate limits of what now is Bay City; James received a part of what later became East Saginaw, and Peter's land covered what later became Carrollton Township. None of the Rileys ever took up permanent residence here, and later sold the land. Their names, however, still appear on abstracts of property as original owners.

The treaty set up reservations for the Indians, but in later agreements these were wiped out, and the Indians received certain lands in Isabella County, still reserved to their use.

Louis Campau remained in Saginaw until 1826 when he moved westward and settled in Grand Rapids. He was succeeded here by Antoine Campau, a relative, who carried on the fur business. Louis bought a large tract of land in the very heart of Grand Rapids, and became one of the founding fathers of that city.

Gen. Cass remained as military governor of Michigan Territory until 1831 when he resigned to become secretary of war under President Andrew Jackson. He left his name in countless places in Michigan — Cass Avenue in Saginaw, Cass County, and at least one high school has been named for him — Cass Technical High in Detroit.

CHAPTER 5

FORT SAGINAW

Once the treaty was signed, the United States Government began to sell land to settlers. This angered the Indians. They realized, for perhaps the first time, the spoken word of the white man, assuring them they could continue hunting in the forests, and the written word, which gave title to the land to the Government, could carry two different meanings.

Although Gen. Cass had said the Indians could go to and from their wigwams without interference, the white settlers did not want Indians walking across their property.

The Indians became unruly, and frightened the settlers. Pressure was put on the government by the settlers for protection, and in 1822 the government decided to establish a military fort at Saginaw.

On May 22, 1822, Gen. Winfield Scott sent an order to Col. Ninian Pinckney of the Third Infantry at Green Bay, Wisconsin, to select two companies and go to Saginaw. Col. Pinckney chose Maj. Daniel Baker to head the force. Maj. Baker was told the quartermaster at Detroit would send the nails, hinges, locks, glass and other articles necessary for the houses for the soldiers. The Green Bay soldiers were told to take seeds with them in order to grow the vegetables they would need.

Early in June, the schooner Superior was loaded with supplies at Green Bay. Several of the men took along their wives and children. The schooner stopped at Mackinac Island, in the Straits of Mackinac, to exchange some articles of clothing. About June 18 the ship entered the Saginaw River.

Maj. Baker selected the fort's location at what now is Court and Hamilton Streets, where the Hotel Fordney now stands. The fort was about 200 feet wide and 350 feet long. It was on the river shore and a high bank plunged steeply to the water's edge.

The fort was built of heavy hardwood posts or pickets, mostly oak, cut on three sides. These posts were set deeply into the ground. They stood ten feet high above the ground and were tied together by stout strips of oak bark. There were two main gates. One opened on what is now Michigan Avenue. The second opening, known as the water gate, was toward the river. These gates were 12 feet wide and 12 feet high. The soldiers made certain if an Indian tried to climb over, it would be a difficult climb.

But it wasn't the Indians that gave the soldiers trouble.

Summer evenings in Michigan today can be made troublesome by mosquitoes. Imagine what it was like in 1822! The mosquitoes bred by the millions in the swampy lands along the river, and there was no protection against them. At night a person might hide his head under a blanket, but on a hot night this was almost as unbearable as the mosquito's sting.

The mosquitoes infected the soldiers with malaria, then termed "ague," or merely the "fever." Soon reports were reaching Detroit that the Saginaw fort was an unhealthy location. This report arrived at a time when men of wealth were eyeing the wilderness around Saginaw as a likely spot for development of a town.

Many men were busy buying land and selling it to easterners who wanted to move to the frontier. These businessmen feared that reports of sickness at Saginaw might frighten off their prospective land buyers. So the reports were concealed, and the Saginaw area continued to be advertised as a healthy place to build a new life.

These land speculators were helped with their story by nature. As Winter came on, the swamps froze, the mosquitoes disappeared, and there was no sickness. All Winter the government land surveyors were busy. There was little for the soldiers to do other than drill, keep warm, and shoot enough game to keep fresh meat on the table. The Indians had no thought of making war.

When Spring came, back came the mosquitoes and the fever. The soldiers protested so loudly about being kept at Fort Saginaw that the government finally gave in. When Detroit learned the fort was to be abandoned, the land speculators became alarmed and sent a letter to the Secretary of War, John C. Calhoun, saying:

"The flourishing village of Saginaw is beautifully situated, and the health of the inhabitants is equal to any village in the territory." It also added that within five years Saginaw would be the capital of Michigan.

This "flourishing village" flourished only in the minds of those businessmen who had land to sell. The real facts were told in a letter from a Capt. Garland to the commanding general, Department of the East:

"Sir: It is my duty to apprise the Commanding Officer of this Department that this garrison is now in a most deplorable situation. Maj. Baker and Lt. Baker are both dangerously ill of remittant fever. All the officers belonging to the command are sick except myself. The doctor was so much indisposed this morning as to make it necessary for me to send to Detroit for a physician. There are scarcely enough well men left to take care of the sick."

Dr. John L. Whiting of Detroit went to Fort Saginaw in answer to the plea for medical help. He found the fort's regular physician, Dr. Pitcher, so ill he had to be carried to the bedside of his patients. Even Dr. Whiting came down with the fever after spending three weeks at the fort.

The order to abandon the fort was signed Sept. 16, 1823, and sent from Headquarters on Governor's Island, New York, by Indian runner. The orders reached Fort Saginaw in October, and on Oct. 26 the soldiers boarded a ship on Saginaw River and sailed for Detroit. Saginaw's days as a military outpost were at an end.

The fever the soldiers suffered was not a fatal one. There were two deaths at the fort during the year, but these resulted from typhoid fever. Although settlers also suffered from the malarial fever, the sickness was not bad enough to drive them out of the Saginaw Valley. Fort Saginaw was completely abandoned in 1824, and in the spring of that year it was sold to Samuel W. Dexter, for whom Dexter in Washtenaw County is named. Dexter deeded to Saginaw County the land on which the Court House stands, and designated the property on the northwest corner of present Court and Michigan as "commons." This deed has prohibited the County from selling this land or building on it.

CHAPTER 6

ALEXIS DE TOCQUEVILLE

As late as 1830, the Saginaw area had not felt the heavy hand of civilization to any extent. There were some scattered cabins of white men. The small settlement of Saginaw hugged the river shore and activity was confined largely to the trading post.

Fifteen miles down the river toward Saginaw Bay another settlement was beginning to take shape. It was known as Lower Saginaw. Now it is known as Bay City. No roads led to these settlements. Only men on horseback or foot could travel to them in the spring or summer. In the winter they could go by sled over the frozen surface of the rivers.

By this time, Detroit and Chicago were major midwestern cities. But along the Saginaw, the mosquito, massaga rattlesnake, wolf, panther, bear and deer far outnumbered the humans. Into this wilderness came a young French nobleman, Alexis de Tocqueville, for the purpose of gathering material for a book.

De Tocqueville first visited Detroit, then a city of 3,000 persons. He asked a Maj. Biddle, the government agent for sale of wild lands, where he should travel to get the best look at Michigan.

"There is a settlement at Pontiac," Biddle said, "but beyond that the country is covered by forests so thick you would get lost. It is full of nothing but wild beasts and Indians."

Maj. Biddle suggested that De Tocqueville go west to St. Joseph, but the chance of visiting a wilderness was more than the Frenchman could ignore. He followed the military road as far as it went — Pontiac. At that time, Pontiac had twenty houses, some stores, and two inns. All of this nestled in a square mile of cleared land. De Tocqueville, and his companion another Frenchman, who also published a book entitled "Marie," in which he, too, described the Saginaw area, stayed overnight at one of the inns. They soon had the innkeeper in conversation.

"Ever get preachers up this way?" De Tocqueville asked.

"Once in a while," the innkeeper said. "Almost every summer some Methodist minister appears. The news is passed around from house to house and on the day he is to preach there's quite a crowd. Arrival of a minister is a great event."

De Tocqueville leaned back in his chair. "We want to get up to Saginaw."

The innkeeper was horrified. "You want to go to Saginaw? A foreign gentleman, an intelligent man, wants to go to Saginaw? Impossible."

"Why?" De Tocqueville asked.

"But are you aware what you undertake?" the innkeeper said. "Do you know that Saginaw is the last inhabited spot northwest to the Pacific? That between this place and Saginaw lies an uncleared wilderness? Do you know that the forest is full of Indians and mosquitoes? That you must sleep at least one night under damp trees? Have you thought about the fever?"

But De Tocqueville was insistent. Finally the innkeeper told him which trail to take. By evening of the next day, De Tocqueville and his companion and guides were five miles south of what now is Flint.

"The silence of the forest was so deep," De Tocqueville wrote, "the calm so complete, that the forces of nature seemed paralyzed. No sound was heard but the annoying hum of the mosquitoes and the stamp of our horses' feet. Now and then we saw the distant gleam of a fire, against which we could trace, through the smoke, the stern and motionless profile of an Indian."

The sound of an animal barking echoed through the woods, and the party hurried toward the sound. Soon they came upon a log cabin, separated from them by a fence. De Tocqueville started to climb the fence when out of the moonlight reared a big black bear. It was chained, but was very close, and waved its huge forelegs as if wishing to embrace the intruder.

"What an infernal country," De Tocqueville snorted, "keeping bears for watchdogs."

A man appeared at the cabin door and looked the travelers over closely. Then he turned to the bear. "Go to bed, Trink.

They are not robbers." The man then invited the travelers to spend the night in his cabin.

The next day De Tocqueville hired two other Indians to guide his party to Saginaw. They arrived on the bank of the Saginaw River after dark. The guides signaled three times with savage yells, then pulled their blankets around them to keep off the mosquitoes, and settled down on the river bank to wait. In a few minutes there was a faint noise, and an Indian canoe approached the bank.

The man in the canoe wore the dress and had the appearance of an Indian. He spoke to the guides, who took the saddles from the horses and put the saddles in the canoe. As De Tocqueville prepared to step into the canoe, the man tapped him on the shoulder and said pleasantly:

"Ah! You are from old France — don't be in a hurry. People sometimes get drowned here."

If De Tocqueville's horse had spoken to him he couldn't have been more surprised. He looked at the man, whose face shone in the moonlight like a copper ball.

"Who are you? You speak French, but you look like an Indian."

"I am Bois-Brule, which in your language means the son of a Canadian and an Indian woman."

De Tocqueville settled himself in the bottom of the canoe. In one hand he held the bridle of his horse. As the canoe slipped through the water, the horse swam alongside. Then the canoe returned to the other side for other members of the group.

"All my life I shall remember the second time the canoe neared the shore," De Tocqueville wrote. "The full moon was just rising over the prairie behind us, half the disk appeared on the horizon. It looked like a mysterious door through which we could catch a glimpse of the light of another world.

"It's rays were reflected in the stream and touched the place where I stood. Along the line of the pale light the Indian canoe was advancing. The bark glided rapidly and smoothly, long, narrow and black, resembling an alligator in pursuit of its prey. Behind came the horse, his powerful chest throwing up the waters of the Saginaw in glittering streams. In the whole scene there was wild grandeur which made an impression that has never been forgotten."

Thirty persons — men, women and children — lived at Saginaw at that time. Within two or three years the town would begin to take shape, and this place which De Tocqueville described as "the western most outpost of a far flung civilization" would assume the role of the "lumber capital of the world."

De Tocqueville's visit never was forgotten in Saginaw. When the present East Side Post Office was built it was designed after De Tocqueville's ancestorial chateau in France, perhaps the only post office in the United States to so honor a casual visitor to a wilderness outpost.

CHAPTER 7

PIONEER FARMING

"One for the blackbird, one for the crow,
"One for the cutworm, and three to grow."

Today the Saginaw Valley is one of the richest farm areas in the nation. It is known as the "Bean Pot" of the world, because most of the navy beans eaten in the United States are grown in its rich soil.

But it wasn't always so.

In Saginaw's early days, the little jingle quoted above was the discouraging plaint the farmers used to describe their troubles. Most of the early farmers came from eastern United States, where soil conditions were different than found here. At first they tried to apply eastern farming methods to the Saginaw area. These failed. It took a lot more than a plow and harrow to prepare this soil, and when a crop did appear there were the birds.

Albert Miller began farming on his little clearing at Green Point in 1833. He planted his first crop on March 27, and it came up well. Through early spring and summer it gave promise of yielding enough corn to eat and in addition some to sell.

"Just as the corn was ready to pick," Miller said, "clouds of blackbirds came from the marshes and in spite of all our efforts destroyed the whole crop. From thirty acres of corn, which would have given fifty to sixty bushels of corn to the acre, we saved only the butts of the ears the birds could not reach."

To fight off the birds, the farmers built scaffolds in the fields and children sat there to yell at the birds when they appeared. Ephraim S. Williams and his brother, B. O. Williams, at one time shot into a mass of birds swirling over a cornfield. Boys picked up the dead ones — a total of 545.

Some farmers grew wheat. But there was no mill in Saginaw to grind the grain into flour. The wheat had to be taken to Flushing, near Flint. If this mill couldn't handle the wheat, the farmer had to go on to Pontiac. It could be a 10-day trip to mill and back.

The Saginaw pioneer farmer ate wild game, pork, bread and potatoes, plus whatever vegetables he could raise. In addition to raising crops, he kept busy piling and burning trees and brush and uprooting stumps. Next to his plow the most important implements he owned were his gun and ax.

There were more sheep than any other type of livestock. Some hogs were kept to discourage the rattlesnakes. Almost every farm had a cow. Oxen were used for farm work because they were cheaper to feed than horses and also could be eaten if the going was too bad.

The farms were far apart, and the social life revolved around barn raisings, corn huskings, and other "bees" that drew families together. Land was cheap, only $1.25 an acre, but it was hard to clear. After the trees had been cut, the farmer had to pull the stumps and roots.

The pioneer plow was a big thing made with a large white oak beam. If it was made properly by a blacksmith it could cut through four or five inches of solid oak root.

The log houses the pioneers built had wall-to-wall dirt floors. Living was centered around a large open fireplace with its iron crane and pot hooks for cooking. Light came from a pan of grease with a coiled rag as a wick. Standard household articles were the butter churn, spinning wheel, yarn-winder, wash tubs and refuse buckets.

Rattlesnakes were plentiful. Farmers at work wore heavy boots that came high up on the leg. One farmer set out to move a pile of branches. As he pulled one branch out, he uncovered a rattlesnake. More branches were pulled and more rattlers slithered to the ground. The entire pile seemed filled with snakes. The farmer walked away. Moving the pile could wait until the snakes moved out.

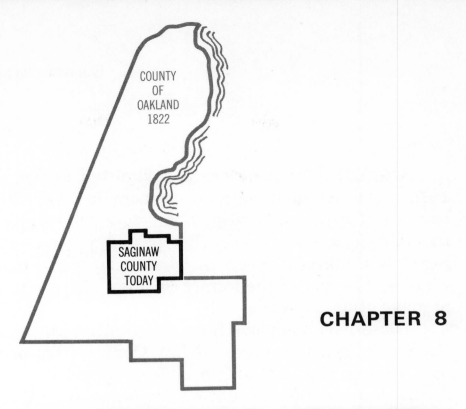

COUNTY
OF
OAKLAND
1822

SAGINAW
COUNTY
TODAY

CHAPTER 8

SAGINAW COUNTY IS FORMED

There's nothing very romantic about the formation of a county or a township. Unlike cities, which are built by men, counties and townships are formed by some higher government by decree.

But Saginaw County wasn't always its present size. On Sept. 10, 1822, Gen. Lewis Cass by proclamation declared that the County of Saginaw shall be attached to and composed of part of the County of Oakland.

In 1830 the Territorial Government of Michigan passed a law which formed a new County of Saginaw and its boundaries stretched to the Straits of Mackinac. In 1831 another law was passed giving Saginaw County 32 townships, and the boundaries under this law included portions of present day Gladwin, Midland, and Tuscola Counties. Saginaw was the county seat.

Although Michigan was not admitted to the Union until 1837, it had adopted state government in 1835 when the first state constitution was ratified and state officers elected. It was the 1835 state government that passed a law creating a new Saginaw County of pieces of what today helps make up Bay County. The rest of the former Saginaw County was cut away to make other counties.

These 1835 boundary lines stood until Feb. 17, 1857, when the State Legislature created Bay County from parts of Saginaw, Arenac, and Midland Counties — provided it was approved by the electors of those counties. Saginaw and Midland residents voted against this plan. But Bay County residents took the matter to court, and the ruling was that the votes of persons living within the boundary lines of the proposed Bay County should count more than those outside. Bay County was formed as a unit of government in 1858.

Saginaw County thus was trimmed down to the boundary lines it owns today. Meanwhile, townships had been organizing within the county. Saginaw Township was the first to organize. It had its first meeting on April 4, 1831. Marion Township was the last, it organized in 1880. There are 27 townships in Saginaw County, and each elects a supervisor. The county is governed by a board of supervisors which meets regularly throughout the year and passes laws for the county much after the fashion of a Legislature or a City Council.

CHAPTER 9

THE CITY IS BORN

In 1822, the year Fort Saginaw was built, two men, Dr. Charles Little and his son, Norman, came from New York and made their way through the forest to Saginaw.

Both were dreamers, and what they saw pleased them. They could see a city where only pine trees grew, and their name was forever to be associated with Saginaw. Dr. Little bought many acres of land on both sides of the Saginaw River. Then he and his son went back to New York.

That same year, two other men came to Fort Saginaw. One was Capt. James Farley, the other was James McCloskey. These men were dreamers, too. They surveyed and purchased from the government 136 acres of land. This was to become the center of what now is the west side of Saginaw.

Later McCloskey sold his holdings to Dr. Little. Farley kept his. The government sold the fort and its property in 1825 to Samuel W. Dexter, of Washtenaw County. In 1830 Dexter had his holdings surveyed and platted, and gave it the name of Saginaw City. It was a name only.

It does not appear that Farley, McCloskey or Dexter ever were residents of Saginaw. They purchased land for speculation or development, and sold later at a profit. Making a profit on frontier land was not difficult. The entire nation was seized with the idea that the west was going to grow rapidly and land in the wilderness began to sell faster and faster. As it sold, prices went up. And as prices went up more men were infected by the get-rich fever. Men in New York, who never went farther west than the Hudson River, would map out towns in the wilderness and then sell lots to eager easterners who wanted to move west. It was one of the maddest periods in early American life.

In 1835, Dexter sold his land in Saginaw to Dr. Millington of Ypsilanti for $11,000. The next year, Norman Little returned to Saginaw, determined to build the city his father had dreamed about. He had financial backing from the firm of Mackie, Oakley & Jennison of New York. Norman Little was a promoter, one of the best. Before he returned to Saginaw, he flooded the east with advertisements about the charms of Saginaw. Prospective settlers were told they couldn't find a better place to live; that within a few years there would be a deep water canal connecting Saginaw with Lake Michigan. This canal, the handbills shouted, was to make Saginaw the leading port city of all the Great Lakes.

Little arrived in 1836 in grand style. He came overland to Detroit. There he chartered the steamboat, Governor Marcy. This he loaded with important Detroit businessmen and some

settlers. The steamboat arrived here in July, and caused a lot of excitement. It was the first steamboat to be seen on the Saginaw River.

Little set out to build his city by buying up lands his father had failed to buy earlier. Dr. Millington, who in 1835 had purchased all of Dexter's holdings, calmly asked Little $55,000 for his properties and got it. Little had a new map made of the city. This one included 407 blocks, and on paper it looked fine.

By the end of 1837, Saginaw City had 900 residents. Meanwhile, Little and his backers decided the new city needed a hotel. The Webster House, on the corner of what now is Michigan and Cleveland, was built. It was big enough to meet the hotel needs of a town of 10,000. For a long time it was the grandest hotel in all of Michigan — and the emptiest.

Inflation hit its peak in 1838. What happened in Saginaw was happening all over the nation. Land prices zoomed. One 80-acre plot within a mile of the Saginaw River sold $80,000. More than a mile stretch of land to the south of Fort Saginaw was mapped out. Buyers, however, were not told the land was covered with water the year around and heavily populated with frogs, muskrats, and swamp weeds.

Buildings went up in Saginaw City in this period. Stores appeared. Warehouses were built. Banks opened and issued their own money — paper bills with "promise to pay in silver" printed on them. The money was not backed by the U.S. Government, and was as good only as the bank that issued it. Even Zilwaukee, which was little more than a fur trading post, had a bank that issued money. One of the Zilwaukee bank's notes was a three-dollar bill, one of several banks that issued such bills during this period.

The panic came in 1838. The good times faded. The people realized with a sickening feeling the bills they had accepted in payment for goods or had received as wages were worthless. Depression had come to the United States, and it set the development of Saginaw back many years. For a long time the business of the nation was paralyzed as a result of the wild speculation.

Saginaw City changed from a bustling center of trade to a farming village. Those who stayed did so because they had no money and no place to go. Those who had places to go left. On April 9, 1841, Little and his associates sold out all of their holdings on both sides of the river for $200,000. This was a mere fraction of the sum they had poured out in their efforts to build a city. Little went back east.

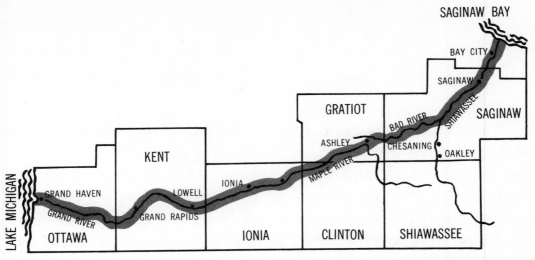

CHAPTER 10

THE GRAND CANAL

Sometime in 1836 this advertisement appeared in eastern newspapers.

"The City of Saginaw lies in the heart of Michigan at the head of steamboat navigation on the Saginaw River, which is formed by the Flint, Cass, Shiawassee, and Tittabawassee Rivers. The Shiawassee may easily and doubtless soon will be connected by a short canal with the Grand River, by which trade of all that country and much from the eastern shore of Lake Michigan will center at Saginaw."

The idea was to build a big ship canal across the middle of Michigan, following the route carved out by the glacial spillway. It would follow the course of the Bad River to Maple River, then to Grand River, which empties into Lake Michigan. This would permit ships to sail from Chicago to Saginaw and Detroit by way of Saginaw Bay, a much shorter voyage than by way of the Straits of Mackinac.

The scheme was approved by the State of Michigan. The first Legislature wanted to do something to make the state attractive to settlers, and the Saginaw-Grand Canal was one of the public improvement projects approved.

Norman Little helped push the idea. Early in 1837 surveys were made and specifications prepared for the first section of canal, which would run west from Bad River. Little was given one of the contracts for grubbing and clearing the route. A crew of 100 Irish immigrants was hired and the work began.

Getting supplies to the men was as tough a job as digging the canal. The trail to the construction site, about 25 miles west of Saginaw, was through the same heavy forest that the canal was to run. Many trees were cut by the crew and dams were built. The canal, as planned, was to be 20 miles long, 90 feet wide, and nine feet deep in this particular section.

The work continued until July 1838 when it suddenly stopped. The panic had hit, and the State no longer could make payments for the canal job because The Morris Canal & Banking Co. which had promised to loan the state $5 million for the project had failed.

The Irish workmen didn't get paid and lost their Irish tempers. They came to Saginaw and for three days paraded the streets threatening all they thought had anything to do with the canal. But once the Irishmen realized they weren't going to get paid because there was no money, they left to find jobs elsewhere.

In the less than two years of work on the canal, the state spent $22,256. Ten years later, in 1849, the state approved incorporation of a company composed of Gardner D. Williams, James D. Fraser, and D. J. Johnson of Saginaw to complete the canal. The company was known as the Saginaw & Grand River Canal

Co. It put $200,000 worth of stock on the market to raise money to finance the project. The stock didn't sell and the company failed. So, too, died dreams of a ship canal across Michigan.

Remains of this canal still are visible. Travelers from St. Charles to Brant, in Saginaw County, will notice on their left, just crossing the South Branch of the Bad River, a straight stretch of stream about three-quarters of a mile long. This is all that remains of the work of 100 Irishmen.

CHAPTER 11

CITY OF THE SWAMP

For more than a decade following the panic of 1838 the Saginaw region was almost at a standstill. Then in 1849 Norman Little returned, this time with financial backing from Hoyt & Co. of New York. With him came Jesse and Alfred Hoyt, brothers and sons of James Hoyt of the Hoyt Co.

At first Little tried to buy land in Saginaw City for a new development, but the price was too high. So he turned his attention across the river, and the "city that had no reason to be built" materialized.

The east bank of Saginaw River was the most unlikely spot for a city that Michigan could offer. It was low, while Saginaw City was high. It was foul, swampy land. Louis Campau tried to set up a trading post on the east side of the river in 1820, but abandoned it when the Indians refused to trade there. They insisted he confine his work to one location, the site of the 1819 signing of the Treaty of Saginaw.

Harvey Williams had purchased some land south of the present Bristol Bridge in 1836 and built a saw mill. Williams, also, had plans for a city and in 1837 published a plat of the City of Saginaw. This plat ran a mile along the Saginaw River from a point about at the northern edge of present Hoyt Park, and extending back from the river three-quarters of a mile. The depression of 1838 killed this idea, too.

In 1847, Curtis Emerson, who was to become one of the most eccentric of Saginaw lumber barons, purchased the old Williams saw mill on the east bank, and in partnership with Charles W. Grant, began the production of lumber. That same year, Emerson sent to C. P. Williams & Co., Albany, New York, the first full shipload of clear pine ever shipped from Michigan. A settlement sprang up around the mill, and Emerson named it Buena Vista. The town was organized in April 1849, and Emerson elected supervisor.

Little purchased 2,400 acres of land which covered what now is the East Side Business district. The property did not go as far south as Emerson's sawmill settlement of Buena Vista. Little's acres were largely swamp, which was in turn part of a massive swamp that began in what is now South Saginaw and extended the entire distance through what is now the East Side business district. Today's Hoyt Park bowl was part of this swamp.

Apparently overcoming the obstacles nature threw in his path only made Little more determined. He realized that if he was to populate his new city, he had to have a road through the forest for settlers to travel. There was a road of sorts connecting Saginaw to Flint. The Military Road to Flint had been cut through the forests in 1822, but it wasn't passable for wagons until around 1836.

Little wanted a good road, and in those days a good road was a plank road. Besides, the road available crossed the Cass River at Bridgeport by scow, then followed, roughly, present South Washington Road to the foot of Mackinaw Street, where a ferry boat took the travelers across the river to Saginaw City.

Little applied to the State Legislature in 1848 for a charter to build a new road of wooden planks from Saginaw to Flint, a distance of 32 miles. The legislators were shocked.

"Build a plank road to Flint — through the wilderness? Nonsense!" they snorted. "Might as well build a road to the moon."

But Little didn't give up easily. He got the charter. The Genesee Plank Road was started in 1850, and a sawmill was built to saw the planks for it.

While waiting for the road, Little went ahead with plans for the city. He kept surveyors busy and in 1850 announced the first mapping of East Saginaw. His map was known as Hoyt's Plat and included the area bounded on the north by Astor Street, on the east by Second Avenue, on the south by Emerson Street, and on the west by the river.

Because of the plank road and because there was no river for settlers to cross, East Saginaw grew faster than Saginaw City. The forest surrounding the clearing at the heart of the city was cut away and as the acres were cleared and filled in at least partially they were subdivided into lots. It was a strange appearing town. Pine board sidewalks were laid on pilings over the swamp water, and many a store's backdoor opened onto water. More than one merchant could fish out of the backdoor of his store when business was slow.

With the plank road, however, things began to happen. Stage coaches came from Flint. Soon a post office was estab-

lished. Then a flour mill. Every day, the people would look down the road for the first sight of the wagons bearing more settlers.

"Still they come!" was the cry of the day.

It wasn't until 1852 that Little was confident his new city was here to stay. East Saginaw was incorporated as a village in 1855 with Little as the first president. In 1857, Saginaw City was incorporated as a city with Gardner D. Williams as first mayor. East Saginaw became a city two years later in 1859. Somewhere, in there, the little settlement of Buena Vista was absorbed by the growing East Saginaw.

Meanwhile, Little built a house on the northeast corner of Fitzhugh and Water Streets and settled back to watch his city grow. He didn't watch it long. On the morning of Nov. 8, 1859, his body was found in the river he loved so well, a victim of accidental drowning at the age of 54.

Little brought the Hoyts to Saginaw, and their name is linked solidly with its history. Alfred was the first postmaster of East Saginaw and in 1852 was elected State Representative. In 1854, he sold his interest to his brother, Jesse, and returned to New York City. Jesse remained. Hoyt Library and Hoyt School are name for him.

East Saginaw prospered. It grew bigger and finer than Saginaw City, its older rival on the west bank. East Saginaw was the first town in America to have streets paved with cedar blocks. It's supposed to be true that many a west sider would fix up his fanciest rig on a summer evening and with his span of horses prancing proudly jog through the dust and ruts of his own city over to East Saginaw just to ride on the fancy cedar block pavements.

East Saginaw also had the Swift Electric Light Co. operating in 1881, and had electricity for street lighting. The light company was one of the show places of East Saginaw, and fanned the rivalry between the two Saginaws. In 1884, Saginaw City had a proposal before the City Council to erect and operate an electric lighting plant. It was vetoed by Mayor Charles L. Benjamin, who later, the story goes, regarded that act as a blunder.

While East Saginaw and Saginaw City were feuding, and rivalry was bitter between the two cities, there were three other settlements, now long gone, that sprang up, flourished and disappeared.

Aaron Penney came out of New York State in 1848 and cleared a farm at what now is Center and South Washington, and became the founder of a village. In 1853, William Gallagher, a land speculator, and his brother, John, purchased Penney's farm and named it Salina. In 1866 Salina was incorporated as the Village of South Saginaw, and had a population of 3,000 persons. It was separated from East Saginaw by a bayou between what is now Hoyt Park and Webber Avenue. This barrier threatened to keep the two from joining, but in 1873, South Saginaw joined East Saginaw, casting its lot for ever with the larger city.

There also was the Village of Florence. This place developed on the west side of Saginaw River opposite the point Genesee Avenue meets the river. It consisted of two parallel streets and 39 lots, and at one time boasted a sawmill, three salt blocks, two brine wells, and a shipyard. Strangely enough the Village of Florence existed on paper until 1940 when the C. K. Eddy & Sons asked the circuit court to vacate the old plat that had been originally filed July 28, 1857.

There also was Melbourne. This place was on the west bank of Saginaw River eight miles downstream from East Saginaw. It developed around a sawmill owned by Wellington R. Burt, perhaps the most famous of all of Saginaw's lumber barons and the richest. Melbourne started in 1864, and by 1870 the mill was among the largest and most complete in the world. It had 45 houses for families, two boarding houses, stores, library, and a school. It burned in 1876, and never was rebuilt.

Meanwhile, leaders of East Saginaw and Saginaw City realized the rivalry between them could not be allowed to continue. Prosperity for both towns lay in merger of the two. When consolidation first was proposed, it created such an argument that leaders felt it useless to let the people vote on the proposition.

One of the bitterest of disputes was over location of the city hall. Both sides wanted it. So a compromise was worked out. The city hall would be built on a site equally distant from the West Side and East Side business districts. And that is why the city hall stands where it does today.

Civic leaders of the two cities took their problems to the Legislature and asked for a law to consolidate the two cities. This law was passed and became effective June 28, 1889. Then in March 1890, the first election was held. The consolidation was approved, and George W. Weadock, a distinguished attorney and Democrat, was elected as the first mayor of the consolidated Saginaws.

CHAPTER 12

DAYLIGHT IN THE SWAMP

The lumberjacks came west after logging off the New England states, and what they found on the Saginaw made their eyes pop. The forest was so thick, they said it would take a hundred years to cut.

Greedily they attacked the pine and through the far reaches of the rivers that fed logs into the hungry mills at Saginaw, the lumberjacks with their axes let "daylight into the swamp."

Lumbering in the Saginaw country was the biggest, the best, the rowdiest, and the 'jacks boasted they were the toughest. Saginaw was the lumbering capital of the world from 1851 until the pine gave out in the late 1890's, and the city wore its title with a jaunty air.

They say Saginaw is built on forty feet of sawdust, and maybe this is true — in spots. It never has been measured, so far as any living man knows, but there was enough pine lumber sawed in the mills here to make a pile forty times forty feet.

From 1851, when lumbering became serious business, until 1897, the last big year, the Saginaw River floated pine logs that measured out to more than 25 billion feet of lumber, enough to build a million medium sized homes. And just for good measure, Saginaw mills turned out more than five billion shingles, plus staves and hoops for barrels for shipment of salt that became a cousin of the lumber industry.

A foot of lumber is a piece 12 inches square and one inch thick. It is the term of measurement used to tell how many feet of lumber there are in a log, and experienced lumbermen, called scalers, can figure this out to the inch.

The first sawmill in the Saginaw Valley was built in 1828 by Rowland Perry and Harvey Spencer on Thread River at Grand Blanc, near Flint. Another mill was built a year later on the Thread, but closer to Flint.

The first steam sawmill on the Saginaw River was built for Gardner and Ephraim Williams in 1835 by their cousin, Harvey Williams. It was a crude affair, and could cut about 2,000 feet of one-inch boards in a 12-hour day. The mill was located on the river just south of present Mackinaw Street.

The second Saginaw mill was built in 1836 by Harvey Williams, but on the east side of the river just south of Bristol Bridge. This mill operated for eight years, then was shut down. In 1846, it was purchased by Curtis Emerson and Charles W. Grant.

These new owners put new boilers, a new engine, and other new equipment in it and were ready to start making logging

history. The mill was 55 feet long and 12 feet wide, and had a capacity of about three million feet of lumber a year. When Emerson sent the first cargo of lumber by boat out of Saginaw in 1847 to Albany, N. Y., its fine quality attracted attention. Almost immediately there was a demand for Saginaw pine.

The next mill was built in 1850 by Charles W. Grant and Alfred Hoyt. By this time eastern capital had become excited about lumbering prospects on the Saginaw, and money poured in to build more mills. By the end of 1855 there were 23 mills producing 60 million feet of lumber a year.

The growth continued. In 1870 there were 83 mills on the Saginaw River yielding 576,736,000 feet of lumber. In the peak year of 1882 the cut was 1,011,274,905 feet.

Saginaw came rightly by its position as lumber capital of the world. The Saginaw River, formed by the Flint, Cass, Shiawassee, and Tittabawassee Rivers, drains a total of 3,200 square miles from the Michigan Thumb area north and west into Gladwin, Gratiot, Isabella, and Clare Counties. These rivers and their tributaries all poured logs into Saginaw. But the Tittabawassee was the greatest of them all.

This river and its tributaries flow through what was some of the finest pine country in Michigan, and the finest in the nation. The Chippewa River, rising in Isabella County, and the Pine River rising in Gratiot County join the Tittabawassee River at Midland. The Salt River empties into it at Sanford. The Tobacco River joins at Edenville, famous in Michigan lumbering history as Camp Sixteen.

The Cass River valley became famous for its pure quality of pine. This river floated logs that cut into 1,126,000,000 feet of lumber. One of the Cass River's lumbering camps was located on land now occupied by the Tuscola County Court House in Caro.

As the logs floated into Saginaw on the various rivers, they had to be sorted as to ownership. Each log was marked, much as cattle are branded on the prairie ranges. Each logmark was officially recorded so there could be no mistake. The logs were marked on the butt end, of course, but thieves still contrived to steel thousands of them by sawing a few inches off the butt of the log and applying a new mark.

The logs were collected in great booms, and from these booms men would sort out all logs bearing the same logmark. These logs would be tied into rafts and floated down to the Saginaw River and thence to the right mill. Each of the main rivers flowing into the Saginaw had a boom company. The big-

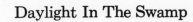

gest of these was the Tittabawassee River Boom Company which handled logs that cut into 11,850,000,000 feet of lumber in its lifetime.

For many years cutting of the timber was done only in winter, and many farmers joined the lumberjacks when they went north with the first snow to work until spring in the lumber camps. Winter was the season for work in the woods for ice roads could be built for great sleds hauling the logs from where they fell to the nearest stream, which would carry them down to Saginaw on the crest of spring floods.

Being a lumberjack was hard work and often boresome. The camps were far back in the woods, away from settlements, and the men very often would not come out of the woods until spring. For entertainment they made up and sang ballads of their life and fellow workers. Often the rhymes were crude, but always they were sentimental and most often very sad. A few have been preserved, but many couldn't stand to live in print.

Life for a lumberjack began early in the morning with a hearty breakfast, and the day was spent in the woods. Some crews would cut the trees, others would trim the branches off and pile them. These piles were called slashings, and they were left as worthless to dry out in the woods and in time became the source of great fires that swept much of the state.

Other crews would roll the logs onto sleds to be carted to the rollways at riverbanks. The ox was the favorite animal of the logger. A team of horses might jerk or pull unevenly, but oxen gave a strong, steady pull that would not dislodge the logs piles on the sled, spill the logs, block the road, and perhaps injure the loaders.

Accidents, of course, did happen, and hospital care was expensive. The nurses at St. Mary's Hospital in Saginaw saw the need for some kind of insurance, and through their ingenuity organized what may have been the first accident insurance of its kind in Michigan history. The nurses would go into the lumber camps and for a modest price sell the lumberjacks hospital insurance, the holders of which could get care at no extra cost at the hospital.

As the forest was pushed back from the streams, railroads laid spur tracks from the river banks into the forests. Much timber was brought to Saginaw by rail, but water transport remained the best and cheapest method.

Banking ground was the name given places where logs were dumped on the river shore, even on the ice, to await the spring

breakup and the floodtime of water. There were two famous banking grounds on the Tittabawassee, and each laid claim to being the world's largest. One of these was at Averill, then known as Red Keg, and the other was at Ox Bow, between Sanford and Edenville. As the logs piled up at the banking grounds they made an awesome sight. The river bank at Red Keg was 30 to 40 feet high and before the ice thawed and the logs began to move downstream, the heap of logs in the river would be at ground level.

As the logs floated down the Tittabawassee they were trapped and held at a place known as Bryant's Trip, by an immense boom that stretched across the river. Bryant's Trip was in Thomas Township, Saginaw County, about three miles upstream, north from present Highway M-46 (Gratiot Road).

It was selected for that point because a bend in the river helped hold back the logs. When logs were needed at the sorting places downstream, the trip was opened and logs floated down to be sorted. There was a minor "trip" at what once was called Brown Bar, near Green Point, but was used chiefly to catch stray logs.

To sort the logs required agile men, quick with the pick and peavy, a tool with a movable hook on it that would clutch a log permitting a man to control its movements. All along the Tittabawassee from Bryant's Trip to the river's mouth, pilings were driven to form pockets into which the logs of the various companies were shoved. The logs were identified by the mark on the butt. When enough logs were in a pocket, they were tied into rafts. The log raft was formed by driving hardwood wedges into the logs and then passing ropes from wedge to wedge to hold the logs in place. These rafts then were towed or pushed by tugboat down the Saginaw to the mills.

As the lumber industry grew so did the inventive genius of the lumbermen. Mills switched from the up and down mulay saw to the circular saw. Thomas Munn of Bay City introduced a double-edging table which trimmed both edges of a board in one operation. Improvement of the saws reduced the amount of waste present in early cutting operations.

The first experiment in the use of a band saw for timber cutting was made by James J. McCormick at Bay City about 1858, but it wasn't successful. It was not until about 1883 that this method was perfected and found general acceptance. The chief advantage of the band saw was its speed and thin blade, reducing the cost of operation and the amount of sawdust. The demand for Saginaw pine grew, the appetite of the mills became enormous, and the pine trees had to be cut faster and faster to keep up with them.

In 1870 one of the most important inventions in Michigan timber history was achieved. Sylas C. Overpack of Manistee came up with what became famous as the Michigan "big wheels." The big wheels were just that, wheels 10 feet in diameter, high enough to ride over the stumps. Each set of wheels could carry up to 4,000 feet of timber at one load.

The advent of the big wheels meant that logging could become a year around job. The big wheels rumbled through Michigan and on into Wisconsin and Minnesota, and then into the great Northwest.

The end of the lumbering in Michigan came with a suddenness that was all but tragic. From the peak year of 1882, the annual cut of timber declined steadily until 1897. The lumber bosses saw the end coming and moved on into Wisconsin and Minnesota, and when they had finished there moved on to the West Coast. With them went Michigan's colorful lumberjacks.

Daylight truly had been let into the Michigan swamps. For a brief period some mill owners tried to keep going on the Saginaw by rafting logs from Georgian Bay and other Canadian points, but it didn't work out. The pine was too far away.

During the 46 years it took to exhaust Michigan's pine, the whine of the saw mill and the cry of "timber" was heard throughout the state. The Saginaw operation, while credited with being the biggest, was one of many. Muskegon was another large center.

So complete was the cutting of the pine that only in rare instances are there any virgin pine left in Lower Michigan. One such stand is at Hartwick State Park near Grayling. Here one still can see the great, majestic tree that thrilled the lumberjack and made fortunes for many a lumber baron.

They had said it would take a hundred years to cut Michigan's pine. Man, aided by fire, did it in less than fifty.

CHAPTER 13

GOLDEN SAWDUST

Timber was gold to the Saginaw Valley.

Thousands of men streamed northward in the fall to work in logging camps, and more were employed in the sawmills from early spring to late fall. Sawmills operated only when the ice was out of the river, simply because the river had to be open for the mills to receive logs. Also, the Great Lakes shipping season closed when Winter froze the river and Saginaw Bay.

Supplying the lumber camps meant business for food merchants. Loggers had astonishingly big appetites, and it took a tremendous quantity of food to keep a lumberjack going all day in the woods. At the start, lumberjack food was not too good, but soon the camp bosses learned the better the food the better the men worked. Good camp cooks were able to pick and choose their jobs.

Beans were popular in all cook houses. Most of the navy beans Michigan lumberjacks ate were imported from Vermont. Saginaw Valley hadn't yet turned to agriculture, and the day when it was to become famous for its navy beans many years distant.

Throughout the northern woods little towns sprang up to supply the lumber camps and the lumberjacks with entertainment and relaxation. These towns flourished for a brief while, then faded into memory as the pine vanished. Among these were the towns of Meredith and Johannesburg, almost forgotten now, but at their prime these were hustling places with stores, churches, schools, and, of course, the inevitable saloons.

Meredith had a dismal end. It withered away and finally a big tobacco company offered a lot in the City of Meredith for a specified number of its famous brand of plug chewing tobacco. Meredith still exists on the map, a tiny town in Gladwin County. Johannesburg, another of Michigan's ghost lumber towns, was near Gaylord in Otsego County. Its end was more commonplace. The town was sold at public auction around 1930.

The lumbering era left descriptive and colorful names to unlikely places. Dead Man's Hill, near Harrison, dates back to the lumber days. The hill was named not because it was so treacherous to travel, but rather for the many dark and evil deeds reportedly done at a lumberjack's entertainment place on it.

Towns such as these developed because there was money to be made in the timber industry and on its fringes. Timberland could be purchased from the government at $1.25 an acre. Men would buy thousands of acres of this cheap land, then make big profits from the timber. Sometimes they made money without cutting the pine.

Early in the 1870's, Wellington R. Burt loaned a man some money and as security took title to a section of timberland at the head waters of Muskegon River, near Houghton Lake. The money wasn't repaid and the land was forfeited to Burt.

Several years later, Burt was busy in his office when a rough, hardy fellow walked in. Burt, who had an imperious way about him, paid little attention to him.

"You got some timber land on the upper Muskegon?" the man asked.

"Yes, and it's for sale," Burt snapped.

"What's the price?"

Still intent on his work and anxious to be rid of the man, Burt shot back: "One hundred thousand dollars."

"That your best price?"

"Yes."

"We'll take it."

Surprised, Burt wheeled in his chair and for the first time really looked at his visitor. "Just who are you, anyway?"

The stranger represented Hackley & Humes of Muskegon, one of the biggest lumber firms on the western side of the state.

There were others who became wealthy because they had sturdy legs.

William Callam, who became one of the best known lumbermen in the Saginaw Valley, was working in the lumber camps and mills in 1857. One day while hauling logs to the Chippewa River he found a beautiful stand of pine trees. Some of the trees towered 80 feet to the first branch. The land was government-owned, and the 23-year-old Callam couldn't understand why. But he remembered the location, and when the sawing season ended he checked at the government land office in Saginaw. The pine still was available.

He set out the next day on foot, and spent a week in the section surveying the land.

"I hadn't seen a soul," he said, "until about four o'clock in the afternoon I saw tracks."

The tracks were those of a horse, and Callam knew they had been made by a land-looker. He realized he had no time to waste if he was going to get those pines and he set off on foot for Saginaw, 60 miles away.

He didn't stop, and staggered into the land office just as it opened the next morning. He picked out 140 acres of the section and bought it at $1.25 an acre. Just as he completed the deal, the land-looker rode up, his horse dripping sweat. Callam had beaten him on foot by about 15 minutes.

Callam then bought six horses, hired 15 lumberjacks, bought supplies, and loaded the whole outfit on a scow. His wife went along to cook for the crew. They poled the scow up the Saginaw, Tittabawassee, and the Chippewa until they reached his timber. The next spring they "drove" over one million feet of pine logs down the same rivers to Saginaw. Logs at that time were worth $10 per 1,000 feet. Callam's endurance had paid a rich dividend.

CHAPTER 14

STRIKE ON THE RIVER

The sawmills along the Saginaw whined and spit sawdust eleven hours a day, until in 1885 the mill workers went on strike for a ten-hour day. It was one of the first labor disputes in the Saginaw Valley, certainly the first that reached such bitterness and violence. It started with the cry of the sawyers:

"Ten hours or no sawdust!"

And it swept upriver from Bay City to reach a climax of anger in Saginaw. Answering the sawyers were the mill owners with: "Work eleven hours a day, or no flour on the table!"

The National Guard was called out. Mill owners, insisting the local governments would be held responsible for damage to their mill properties, forced the city fathers to call in the Pinkerton Detective Agency.

It ended with the capitulation of the mill owners — not to the strikers but to the law of the State. The strike's one importance in history was the fact that it acted as a spur to the Legislature to pass one of its first laws for social reform.

The mill working day was from 6 a.m. to 6 p.m., one hour off for lunch. Pay was not great, even in those days of butter at 16 cents a pound and eggs at 10 cents a dozen.

On July 6, 1885, the employes of several Bay City mills refused to go to work. They demanded a 10-hour day with pay equal to that earned in 11 hours. The demand was rejected. Word came to East Saginaw the strikers would come up the river to get the workers there to join in the strike. The Saginaw Knights of Labor, headed by Thomas B. Barry, was indifferent to the Bay City trouble. However, the next day when dockhands unloading a barge in Saginaw demanded 40 cents an hour, a 10-cent raise, they walked off the job when the demand was refused. Barry then took an interest in the strike.

Four days later, 900 Bay City strikers came to Saginaw on the barge Transport. A group of Saginaw sawyers met them, and they marched to Washington and Genesee Avenues. The Bay City group had thoughtfully brought along a band, and the men quickstepped to the Knights of Labor headquarters to the tune of "Rally Around The Flag, Boys." Later they marched to the various mills and closed them.

The following Monday a force of Pinkerton detectives arrived from Chicago and were sworn in as special deputies. Tenseness gripped residents on both sides of the river. Local offi-

cials, fearing the worst, asked Gov. Russell A. Alger for the services of Company E of the National Guard. Gov. Alger approved, and later also ordered the Flint Blues, Company H of Lansing, and the Alpena Company to Saginaw. The presence of the militiamen helped calm the fears that violence would erupt.

Barry was arrested on a charge of conspiracy. He was arraigned and pleaded innocent, and released on $3,000 bail. By this time, the Saginaw strike was known throughout the entire state. Governor Alger, himself, and his staff arrived. "Law and order must be enforced," the governor declared. "A sufficient force is now on hand to insure the preservation of order. Acts of violence or intimidation will be promptly punished."

Some mill owners began to reach settlements on the 10-hour day demand. Both sides, however, concluded that time alone would produce a final settlement. The situation appeared so calm, that the Pinkertons were dismissed.

Then the Rust, Eaton & Co. mill, at the foot of what now is Rust Avenue, tried to resume operations. The mill got a full crew together willing to work for 11 hours a day. A day or so later, a crowd of 200 men gathered in front of the mill. To preserve order, mayors of both cities ordered police to see that no damage was done to the mill or that anyone was injured.

The last violence of the strike occurred at Webber and Washington Avenues where a detail of police stopped a marching line of strikers and dispersed them. After this the strikers were willing to talk peace. Wellington R. Burt was named as mediator between the strikers and mill owners. Nothing concrete emerged. The men went back to work, some in the 10-hour a day mills, others in 11-hour a day mills.

While all this was going on, the Legislature had been considering a bill that would set a day's work at 10 hours. It was passed a short time after peace came to the Saginaw mills. Meanwhile, the charges of conspiracy against Barry had been dropped quietly. Saginaw went back to its job of cutting the pine.

CHAPTER 15

SALTY SAGINAW

Beneath the State of Michigan there's enough salt to turn the fresh water of the Great Lakes into brine.

Salt no longer is big business here, but when lumber was king, Saginaw was among the nation's leading salt producers. Salt springs, or deer-licks, were well known to the Indians. These were places where briny waters seeped to the surface and provided the wild animals with the salt they craved.

Best known of these salt springs were along the Tittabawassee and Salt Rivers. Dr. Douglass Houghton, state geologist in 1837, spoke about the commercial possibilities of the Salt River springs. An attempt was made, on order of the Legislature, to drill two test wells to determine if salt could be produced commercially from wells near the Grand River, about three miles below the then village of Grand Rapids, and near the mouth of the Salt River in Midland County.

By 1842, the State had spent $15,000 on the two wells, but the attempts were not conclusive. The salt lands of the state were then platted into lots and leased with the right to manufacture salt. However, the law provided a state tax of four cents per bushel of salt (56 pounds) produced. This tax was repealed within a few years.

In 1859 a group of Grand Rapids businessmen asked the Legislature for $10,000 to finance further tests for salt at the Grand Rapids well. The request was denied.

The same year, East Saginaw businessmen who had faith in salt as a business, asked the state to establish a bounty for salt production. A bill was prepared proposing that the state pay ten cents bounty on each barrel of salt.

This sent the legislators into gales of laughter, and one, who thought to make the joke even bigger, moved to make the bounty ten cents a bushel, equal to fifty cents a barrel. Carried away by their humor, the legislators passed it and it became law.

The East Saginaw businessmen didn't waste their time laughing. Jesse Hoyt provided ten acres of land, near present Sixth and North Washington Avenues in Saginaw, for the first well. It was drilled to a depth of 633 feet, where good brine was found.

The company built a plant for the manufacture of salt.

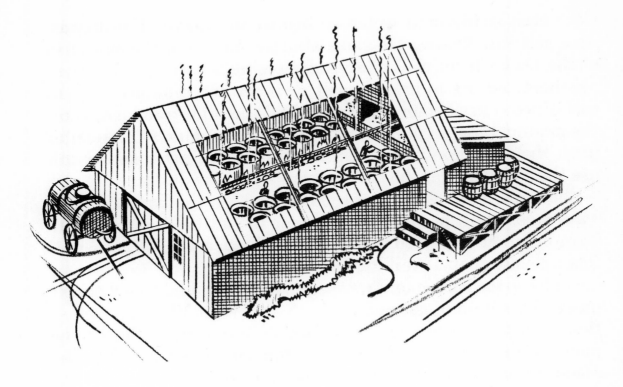

These plants became known as "salt blocks." Wood was used to boil the brine in kettles, and after the water was evaporated salt crystals were left. The production the first year was 10,722 barrels of salt. The second year it jumped to 32,000 barrels.

The Legislature, by this time, had stopped laughing. Without so much as a grin, it repealed the bounty law in 1861. As a result, East Saginaw Salt Manufacturing Co. received only $3,174 in bounty money from the state, and had to go all the way to the State Supreme Court to get that.

The company's success spurred others, and in five years the production of salt here reached 529,000 barrels. Wells were drilled in Saginaw, Carrollton, Bay City, Huron and Iosco

Counties. A Midland well was drilled to 1,300 feet to bring up a rich brine that was to make Midland famous as the location of the Dow Chemical Co. in years to come.

Early efforts to produce salt were not too profitable. The cost of wood needed for the fires to boil the brine was high, and the product brought only a small price on the market. It wasn't until the salt makers and the sawmill owners got together to use the byproduct of the mills — slab wood, sawdust and steam — that salt making became profitable. Not a dollar in profit was made in salt prior to 1870, but for the next 20 years things were different. By 1880 production had reached 2,678,386 barrels, or more than 13 million bushels of salt.

The first salt makers were inexperienced, and based their manufacturing process on New York and West Virginia operations. But the Saginaw brine was different from the brine pumped elsewhere. The Saginaw brine contained iron, which made the salt rusty, bromides of sodium, which made it bitter, and gypsum which made it cake.

To eliminate these impurities, the brine was pumped into big settling tanks built on pilings of lumber. As soon as the tank was filled, fresh-slaked lime was sprinkled over the brine. It was mixed, then allowed to stand for 48 hours until it became crystal clear. The iron, which had a chemical affinity with the lime, was precipitated to the bottom, and the clear brine was drained away.

The first salt was made in kettles. These buildings consisted of two rows of 25 to 30 cast iron kettles each holding 100 to 120 gallons of brine. The building was constructed in such a way as to let the steam escape through the roof. When the brine was boiled about one-third away, the salt was dipped out with ladles into draining baskets, then dumped into salt bins. This was a 24-hours-a-day operation. Each building produced about 27 barrels of salt daily.

Later the pan-block was used. The pans were made of quarter-inch boiler iron. They were from 90 to 120 feet long, 10 to 12 inches deep, and 12 to 15 feet wide. As the brine stood in the pans, small bits of rancid butter were dropped on top. This formed an oily film, and the salt formed beneath it in even crystals. Without the film, the crystalization would not have been uniform.

Another method was known as "solar manufacture," in which the sun did the work. These solar-blocks covered more ground. Shallow wooden vats, 16 by 18 feet in size and six to eight inches deep, were built on foundations two to three feet above the ground. Each vat had a cover which could be used to protect the brine in case of rain. No lime was used in this process because of the different conditions. The iron content was precipitated by the long exposure to the air.

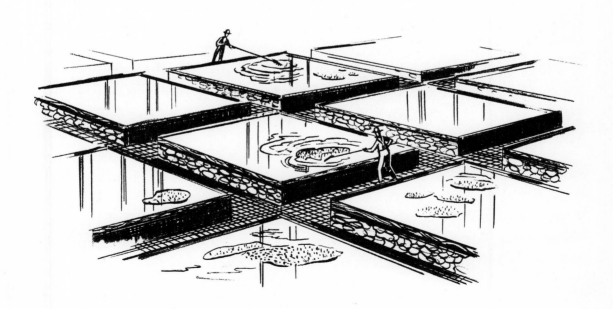

The time required to produce salt in this matter depended on the weather, usually from six weeks to two months. There were three crops a season, the first about the middle of July, the second in early September, and the last late in October. The second crop was generally considered the best, as the crystals were the largest and much in demand by meat packers. But the solar method was too slow, and by 1888 had almost disappeared from use.

In 1888 there were six salt districts in Michigan. Saginaw County led with 1,050,265 barrels of salt. Bay County produced 805,834 barrels. Others making lesser amounts were Huron County, St. Clair County, Iosco County, Midland County, Manistee County, and Mason County. The total amount of salt produced in Michigan from the start of the industry to Jan. 1, 1889, was 45,180,123 barrels.

When the lumber era ended, the salt age all but died, too. There were attempts to keep salt-making alive in the Saginaw Valley by using heat from locally mined coal, but this method could not match the cheap fuel from the sawmills. The Saginaw salt industry died because salt became too expensive to make.

But brine wells continue to pump today throughout the Valley. Not to make salt, but to produce chemicals at the great Dow Chemical Co., Midland. The Dow firm has a network of brine wells throughout this entire area, and pipes run from the wells to the Dow plant.

CHAPTER 16

THE RED SASH BRIGADE

A spirit of adventure was in Saginaw the Lumber Capital. It was in the whine of the saw slicing through a giant pine, the grace of men balancing delicately on logs in the big booms, working with pick and peavey, and the busy toot-toot of the steamboats as they moved down the Saginaw River with their barge tows laden with pine for the world.

Water Street (then Tilden) was paved with sawdust. The sidewalks were of clear white pine plank. Cedar blocks formed the pavements over which the lumber barons drove their beautifully matched teams of horses drawing carriages with the fancy fringe on the top.

In the spring the pine forests sent not only the logs to Saginaw, but the lumberjacks, too. Big, burly men who worked hard, played hard, and fought for the love of it. They came to Saginaw by train to the Pere Marquette Station on Potter Street, and Saginaw welcomed them.

Among these lumberjacks were French-Canadians who wore a red sash about their waists, and the public, always quick to put a nickname on, soon called the annual trek of lumberjacks to the city the "Red Sash Brigade."

It was the mark of a good man to be able to fight, and anyone could get a fight by standing on a street corner and bellowing: "I can lick any man in town." He always got his chance to prove it.

It took some equally tough policemen to handle these men fresh from the woods and hunting for excitement after a dull winter in the logging camps. Patrick Kain and Timothy Mc-Coy, who later became chiefs of the Saginaw Police Department, were two who helped keep the peace. When it became necessary they would move in, whack a few heads with their night-sticks, then trundle the unconscious lumberjacks off to jail.

Saginaw turned out another product besides pine in those days. There was buried in the soft, resilient sawdust piles that bordered the river a disease known as "footlight fever," and for a time Saginaw was known as a great producer of theatrical talent.

There was chubby Leila Koerber, who attended the Hoyt Grade School. She would grow up to become Marie Dressler and a great actress. George Lavigne worked in a sawmill and boxed on Saturday nights. He was to become the famous Saginaw Kid, lightweight champion of the world from 1893 to 1899. Young Tim McCoy watched his father handle the lumberjacks. He was to grow up to become a great star of the Western movies.

Fred Jenks practiced falls on the sawdust piles, and became so adept at making others laugh at his antics he became producing clown for the Ringling Brothers, Barnum & Bailey Circus. He teamed up for awhile with another Saginawian, Harry Watson, and they are credited with originating the now famous clown band that no circus is complete without.

Watson, however, went on to entertainment heights with another sawdust product, George Bickel. This team starred in early Ziegfield Follies, and were world famous. There were others, the Picard Brothers went on to be aerialists in the circus, and the Thomas family adopted the name of the Flying Melzoras and thrilled thousands with their breath taking trapeze stunts under the big top.

The Academy of Music, one of the finest vaudeville houses in the country, opened in Saginaw on Dec. 16, 1884, and the famous of the entertainment world came to Saginaw. The Academy was destroyed by fire in April 1917 and wasn't rebuilt. It's probably just as well. The vaudeville that made it famous was doomed to die anyway.

The lumber barons, the men whose lumbering and mill operations brought them wealth, were in a class of their own. They had money and they spent it lavishly. In 1859 the Hotel Bancroft had its formal opening. It was a grand affair, and the best people in Saginaw and Bay City were invited. A chef was imported from Paris, and the guests came glittering in jewels, fine dresses, white ties and tails.

But Curt Emerson didn't get an invitation. Curt was a boss logger, too, and he reportedly brooded about this seemingly obvious oversight. As he brooded, he got an idea. When all of the guests were assembled in the great dining room, Curt entered. Lightly he sprang to the top of the dining table, and then walked the entire length kicking crystal, drinks, and centerpieces right and left. The next day he happily paid for all the damages.

Then there was Little Jake, the Barnum of merchants.

Little Jake Seligman stood less than four feet eleven. He came to Saginaw in 1872, and his arrival couldn't go unnoticed. He dressed in loud checkered suits, matching ties, and yellow shoes. He sported a black moustache that was carefully waxed and tapered at both ends.

His store was where Heavenrich's now stands. When the lumberjacks hit town he would meet them at the station with a band, and would march them from Potter Street to the store. As the lumberjacks milled around in the street, Little Jake would appear at a second story window and throw a few vests

into the crowd. Any 'jack bringing in a vest would get a free coat and a pair of trousers to match. The fighting over the vests was fierce. Finally a lumberjack would stagger into the store, the tattered remains of a vest proudly held high.

Little Jake kept his word. He gave a coat and a pair of trousers free, but charged the lumberjack $12 for a new vest — which, surprisingly, was the exact cost of the new suit of clothes.

Little Jake didn't confine his activities to his store. He bought the East Saginaw City Street Railway and renamed it the Union Street Railway. He painted the horse drawn street cars red, yellow, and blue. Each color meant a different route.

He also was the only man ever to give his personal statue to the city. He bought the flatiron building at Lapeer, Jefferson and Genesee Avenues for $40,000, and then erected a big clock tower. On top of the clock he put his statue. At least Little Jake said it was a statue of himself, but some doubting Thomases among the residents disagreed. They pointed out that the statue was of a man wearing a hat and a flowing cape, and it looked more like a statue taken from a Civil War cemetery than anything resembling Little Jake.

To prove it was he, Little Jake changed his style of clothes to match the clothes worn by the statue. Later he sold the building, but retained title to the clock and statue. These he deeded to the city. The statue remained until July 24, 1940, when a big wind blew it down. There was some sentiment to restore it, but not enough to raise the money for the job. The late State Senator John P. Schuch, a student of Saginaw history, studied the fallen statue, and concluded it wasn't a statue of Little Jake at all. It was, Schuch decided, a statue from a Civil War cemetery. Eventually the statue came to an ignominious end in a scrap metal collection during World War II.

Of all the lumberjacks whose calked boots pitted the pine sidewalks of Saginaw one has become a great legend. Silver Jack Driscoll is remembered while others are forgotten. Just why the legends grew about Silver Jack isn't clear. He certainly wasn't the Galahad of the pine forests. He spent a considerable part of his life in prison. But, man, how he could fight.

He was a moose of a man, with hams for fists, and some say

the greatest fighter the Michigan forests produced. He was born in Canada about 1845, and he could handle ax and peavey with extraordinary skill. There are many stories about Silver Jack. He was the leading figure in several of the lumber camp ballads sung during the cold, bleak winter nights. But according to a report in The Saginaw Press, there appears agreement on the facts surrounding his fight with Joe Fournier in a saloon at Red Keg (Averill).

Fournier was something of a legend himself. He had a double row of teeth, it is said, and reportedly when he entered a new bar he would sink his teeth into the wood railing and then announce: "Dat's Joe Fournier — hees mark." There wasn't any question when the two bully boys met there would be a fight. There just had to be in order to prove which was the best.

They finally met at Red Keg, and no challenge was necessary. Fournier got a grip on Silver Jack's throat and hung on like a bulldog. Silver Jack's eyes were bulging when Fournier made the mistake of putting one foot on the brass rail. Silver Jack's hobnailed boot stamped on it, and the hold was broken Driscoll landed one punch and the fight was over.

Silver Jack's death has different versions. But the one that appears the most likely is that he died peacefully in bed in 1895 at L'Anse, Wisconsin. Fournier's death was more public. It occurred in 1876 on the sawdust packed deck of the Third Street dock in Bay City when Blinky Robinson hit him over the head with a mallet.

The only sport to come out of the logging camps was log rolling or birling. In this sport two men mount a log in the water and spin it with their feet, each trying to throw the other into the water. It takes quick muscles and great agility, and each camp had its own champion. Contests between the camp champions were arranged at a moments notice. The prize usually was a keg of rum to the winner.

CHAPTER 17

FIRE!

Fire followed the lumberjacks through the forests. Starting in the 1870's and for the next decade, fierce blazes swept the cut over lands of Michigan.

The limbs from the great pine trees were cut off in the forests and piled. These piles of slashings were left as the loggers finished one section and moved into another. Eventually they became tinder dry, and when the time came they burst into deadly flame.

One of the worst fires in Michigan history, and the one that launched the American Red Cross on its program of giving aid to disaster stricken areas occurred in 1881 and swept through three counties Huron, Tuscola, and Sanilac.

The summer of 1881 was unusually dry and hot. During July and August no rain fell. Streams stopped running, wells and cisterns dried up and the dark, mosquito-infested swamps were drained. The stage was set. It only remained for the settlers themselves to apply the torch.

The farmers had taken advantage of the dry spell to burn off the poplar, ash, and maple trees passed over by the lumbermen a decade earlier. For weeks the air was heavy with smoke from these individual fires, and the people became accustomed to the smoke smarting their eyes; so accustomed they lost their fear of fire.

When the great fire started it was not one of those that starts in one place and keeps rolling along by feeding on fresh material, like a grass fire racing over a field. It seemed to go all at once, as if the entire Thumb District was the head of a match and at a signal the match was struck.

On Aug. 31 a fire originating in Lapeer County spread northward to Sandusky in Sanilac County, then north to Deckerville. The wind, that had reached gale proportions, blew out the flames that same night. The fear subsided.

Local histories all speak of the great fire starting shortly before 2 p.m. on September 5, a Monday. By noon the air was thicker with smoke than on previous days, and two hours later a black cloud had blotted out the sun. The winds howled with near hurricane force, and kerosene lamps were lighted in homes.

The fire stopped at the Cass River, sparing Cass City in Tuscola County, but thirty miles to the north at Bad Axe, Huron County seat, a fire was developing near the Huron County poor farm. Suddenly, there was fire every place in the Thumb. There was no place to hide, no place to run. Some people sought shelter in plowed fields, digging holes in the earth to bury heads, meanwhile the fire burned their clothes and blistered their flesh. Some sought safety in the rivers, submerging their heads to escape the cruel flames and heat. The river water became so hot that fish, trapped in the shallows, were cooked. Some people climbed into wells, clinging to the sides with fingers and toes, as the fire raged over and about them.

Wild beasts lost their fear of man. The bodies of one family were found in a cornfield, and nearby was the body of a bear which had sought the company of humans in its desperate end. Another man leaped into Lake Huron and found himself side by side with a big bear, as docile and submissive as a dog.

The intense heat withered the leaves on trees two miles from the fire itself. Fields of corn, potatoes, onions, and other vegetables not touched by the fire were roasted. Fruit orchards burst into bloom, the petals quickly dropping burned and seared.

The flames advanced with the roar of a tornado. Trees were uprooted, buildings blown down, flaming roofs carried through the air, and men and women lifted from their feet and flung back violently. Horses galloping before the flames were overtaken, and left roasting on the ground.

The people prayed and as they prayed they fought with shovels and buckets of water. One woman took her two children to a well, already surrounded by other persons. She covered her children with dirt, and then poured water on them and on herself. When it was over, her dress was pock-marked with holes where sparks had fallen. A hunter, skinning a moose in the forest, was surrounded by flames. No place to go, he got inside the carcass, and pulled the skin tight around him. There he stayed safe, while the fire cooked the outside of the moose.

Along the Lake Huron shore so many ashes fell into the water, the shore water was turned to a lye solution. It was necessary to go several feet below the surface to get fresh water.

The fire burned three days before rain came and drowned it out. The Michigan Fire Relief Commission, sent into the area by Gov. David H. Jerome, made a survey of the damages and supervised relief. The commission reported 1,521 homes and 1,408 barns had been destroyed. There never was an official count of the dead. Some estimates are as low as 125, others as high as 300. The generally accepted figure is around 200.

Clara Barton, founder of the Red Cross, issued a nation-wide appeal for clothing and food for the stricken area. It was the first time the Red Cross had made such a plea for survivors of a disaster.

THE DAY SAGINAW BURNED

Saginaw's greatest fire, which came at the end of the lumbering era here, was not as widespread or as destructive of life as the Thumb fire. But it was vicious. It occurred on May 20, 1893, a warm windy day.

There are various accounts of how the fire started. The only point of agreement is that it started on the middle ground, now Ojibway Island. Robert B. Hudson, a retired fire chief who helped to fight it, said it was due to carelessness of a man who was calking and tarring a boat near the Sample & Camp mill. The man was melting tar over a fire, and the heavy wind blew a spark from the fire to lumber stored at the mill.

Other accounts, all from supposed eye-witnesses, say the fire started from a spark from a locomotive or from a nearby mill that fell into the Sample & Camp mill lumber pile.

Whatever the cause, it did start about 3:30 p.m. The wind

blew flaming embers to the east end of Bristol Street Bridge, which quickly caught fire. Other embers landed among buildings in the block bounded by Washington, Atwater, McCoskry and Water.

As fire built up, the wind increased in violence. The Saginaw Fire Department was unable to contain the flames, and help was asked from Bay City and Flint. Equipment was rushed to Saginaw on railroad flatcars.

The heat was intense. Whole houses in the path of the fire suddenly erupted into flames. Flaming shingles and slab fragments were flung aloft to settle on lumber piles and roof tops. Jefferson Avenue was paved with round cedar blocks held in place by a mixture of sand and gravel. The blocks ignited, and Jefferson Avenue was covered by fiery circles that looked strangely beautiful in the tragic setting.

St. Vincent's Orphan Home was destroyed just after the 49 children had been taken to safety. But St. Mary's Hospital, in the path of the fire, was saved by a twist of fate and an erratic wind. Much of the credit for saving the hospital went to nuns who stood on the roof pouring water on embers blown there by the wind. The hospital was the only major building left standing in the devastated area.

In all, a 30-block area was burned. A total of 239 homes were lost, and 800 persons were made homeless. There was only one death, an elderly man who presumably died of a heart attack brought on by excitement.

The firemen got control of the flames by that evening. The area burned was bounded by the Saginaw River on the west, Franklin and Meredith Street and the Grand Trunk tracks on the northwest, Emerson and Hoyt on the north, Weadock on the east, and Martha, McCoskry and Atwater Streets on the southeast. The total loss by the fire was $670,000 of which $464,-000 was covered by insurance.

As this blaze was dying, the Germain Woodworking plant and planing mill on Holland Avenue caught fire and was destroyed.

CHAPTER 19

THE GRACEFUL DAYS

The lumber barons liked to entertain, and to do it in style they built big and lavish homes. Most of these homes were built in the 1880's and 1890's. Living then was more leisurely than it is today, and hosts and hostesses took time and pleasure in party and dinner preparations.

The parties were beautiful and large. Strains of the lovely Strauss waltzes played by an orchestra carefully concealed behind a bank of palms provided atmosphere at major functions.

This was the horse-and-carriage age when young people danced the waltz and peppy two-step, and spooned as the faithful horse drew the buggy homeward in the sleepy morning hours.

Most of these old homes have disappeared. Their disappearance is as much responsible to the fact that the city has changed as it is to the inescapable fact that no servantless modern housewife would want one of them with their 16 to 30 rooms.

But to understand the homes and appreciate why they were big, step back to 1880. Tonight we'll go to a cotillion. For days preparations for the party have kept the entire household busy. The mistress of the house, a very careful housekeeper who permits smoking only in the smoking rooms, almost forgot to tell the man who brought the white canvas for the floor and stairway to put out his cigar before entering the house.

A group of young people have been invited, and the party is certain to be one of the highlights of the social season. Maids and butlers are scurrying from room to room whisking a dusting cloth over the baseboards and crystal candelabra. The florist with a dray full of palms and American Beauty roses is demanding to know where to put the flowers. Yards and yards of smilax are festooned about the rooms.

Pretty soon Finzel's orchestra will arrive from Detroit. Down at Burton's livery stable the young men will be waiting impatiently for the stable boy to harness their horses. Their partners for the evening are primping carefully and soon will be ready.

The cotillion, a dancing party, was popular at the turn of the century. As each young man made his request to dance with a young lady he would present her with a favor. The host supplied the favors, and they covered a large table in the ballroom. The young women came equipped. Each carried a large purse in which they put the favors. The more dances they had with different young men, the more favors they received. A popular girl could take home a purse full of favors.

Dinner parties also were popular and hostesses worked hours on menus and center pieces to make their tables attractive. It wasn't unusual for a hostess to have a horn of plenty filled with American Beauty roses hanging from the overhead gas light. Generally, only candle light was permitted in the dining room.

And into this soothing atmosphere came the food — oysters on the half-shell, pattie shells filled with chicken or turkey, cranberry jelly, sweet and white potatoes, squash and pickled peaches. For dessert, fruit pudding with hard sauce, ice cream, coffee and nuts.

In the winter the young men entertained themselves with horse racing on the ice. Ice about 20 inches thick would form on the Saginaw River. Rivalry between the two Saginaws was strong, and some of these rivalries were settled on the ice.

Races could be arranged at almost anytime, but for the most part two days each week — Wednesday and Saturday — were set aside especially for racing. There were races for pacers and races for trotters. The half-mile track was swept clear of snow between the present Genesee Avenue bridge and the Chesapeake & Ohio Railroad bridge. Crowds of spectators lined the banks of the river as high spirited horses drew trim cutters over the ice.

Men who were to mature into civic leaders of Saginaw held the reins and accepted any and all challenges. On racing days it was common to see more than 100 horses on the ice. It wasn't professional racing; it was "gentlemen's racing" and no true sportsman would break the rules.

When the river ice wasn't just right, the young men would ice North Hamilton Street or Hoyt Avenue and run their races there. This type of racing died out about 1915, perhaps banished by the rising tide of automobile traffic, and never has been revived.

Politics played an important part in early Saginaw, too. Two men from this era, David H. Jerome and Aaron T. Bliss, rose through the political ranks to become governors of the state.

But with the passing of the lumber and turn of the new century, Saginaw changed. It made the transition, not without depression days and difficult adjustments, from lumber town to industrial city.

Saginaw's first golden era had ended with the fall of the last pine in the once great Saginaw Valley forests.

— the end —

Bibliography

Fred Dustin, "Saginaw History."
Willard Baird, "This Is Our Michigan."
Mills History of Saginaw County.
Dr. George E. Butterfield, "Bay County Past and Present."
Files of The Saginaw News.